RED
from A to Z

(COLOR THE WORD AND EACH SQUARE RED)

APPLE

BLOOD

CHERRY

DARTH MAUL

ELMO

FIRETRUCK

GERANIUM

HEART

INCREDIBLES

JAPANESE FLAG

KETCHUP

LIPSTICK

MERCURY

NOSE (RUDOLPH)

OLD SPICE

COLORS

from A to Z
COLORING BOOK

By: *Matt Weber*

Illustrated by: **An Ant**

RED

YELLOW

PINK

WHITE

PURPLE

GREEN BROWN

ORANGE GRAY

BLUE BLACK

ISBN-13:978-1-949356-03-8

For Caitlin and Samantha, Always be colorful! -Dad

POINSETTIA

QUAKER OATS

RUBY

STRAWBERRY

TOMATO

U.S. FLAG

VOLCANO

WAGON

X-MAS STOCKING

YASTRZEMSKI

ZINNIA

ORANGE...

ORANGE

from A to Z

(COLOR THE WORD AND EACH SQUARE ORANGE)

AMERICAN CHEESE

BASKETBALL

CARROT

DUKES OF HAZZARD

ELWAY

FANTA

GOLDFISH

HOME DEPOT

ICELAND POPPY

JACK-O-LANTERN

KRAFT

LIFE JACKET

MARIGOLD

NEMO

ORANGE

PEACH

QUESO

ROLAND GARROS

SUNSET

TANGERINE

UNIVERSITY OF TEXAS

VEST

WINNIE THE POOH'S BOUNCY FRIEND

X-MAS ORANGE

YIELD SIGN

ZUCCHINI FLOWER

YELLOW...

YELLOW
from A to Z

(COLOR THE WORD AND EACH SQUARE YELLOW)

ANGRY BIRD

BANANA

CANARY

DAFFODIL

EMOJI

FOOTBALL FLAG

GRAPEFRUIT

HIGHLIGHTER

ITOH PEONY

JACKET

KUMQUAT

LEMON

MUSTARD

NINE BALL

ONE BALL

PINEAPPLE

QUINCE

RUBBER DUCKY

SUNFLOWER

TAXI

URINE

VERMONT AVE.

WARBLER

X-MAS BELL

YOLK

ZEST OF LEMON

GREEN...

GREEN
from A to Z

(COLOR THE WORD AND EACH SQUARE GREEN)

AVOCADO

BABY SPINACH

CLOVER

DOUGLAS FIR

EMERALD

FIELD

GOLF COURSE

HILL

IRELAND

JADE

KALE

LIME

MOSS

NIGHTSHADE

OSCAR THE GROUCH

PEA

QUAD

RUTABAGA

SHAMROCK

TRACTOR

UNIVERSITY OF MIAMI

VERNOR'S

WIMBLEDON

X-MAS TREE

YODA

ZINNIA LEAF

BLUE...

BLUE
from A to Z

(COLOR THE WORD AND EACH SQUARE BLUE)

AMERICAN FLAG   BLUEBERRY   COOKIE MONSTER

DORY

EARTH

FACEBOOK

GROUCHY SMURF

HUMPBACK WHALE

INDIGO

JAY

KENTUCKY

LUPIN

MORNING GLORY

NEPTUNE

OCEAN

PICASSO

QUEENSLAND FLAG

ROBIN EGG

SKY

TWO BALL

U.S. OPEN

VACCINIUM CORYMBUSUM

WATER

XANAX

YALE

ZEVIA COLA

GREEN...

PURPLE
from A to Z

(COLOR THE WORD AND EACH SQUARE PURPLE)

AMETHYST

BARNEY

CABBAGE

DATE

EGGPLANT

FIG

GRAPE JUICE

HAROLD'S CRAYON

IRIS

JAM

KING

LILAC

MOUNTAINS MAJESTY

NATASHA FATALE

ORCHID

PANSY

QUEEN

RAISIN

SAGE

THISTLE

URCHIN

VELVET

WILLY WONKA

X-MAS PUDDING

YAHOO!

ZIMMER

BROWN...

BROWN
from A to Z

(COLOR THE WORD AND EACH SQUARE BROWN)

APE

BEAR

CHOCOLATE

DIRTY DIAPER

EARTH

FOOTBALL

GRIZZLY

HAIR

INFIELD

JACKRABBIT

KANGAROO

LEATHER

MUD

NEST

OWL

PEANUT BUTTER

QUAIL

RAPTOR

SOIL

TOOTSIE ROLL

UKULELE

VULTURE

WALNUT

X-MAS TREE TRUNK

YAK

ZITHER

PINK...

PINK

from A to Z

(COLOR THE WORD AND EACH SQUARE PINK)

AMARYLLIS

BUBBLE GUM

COTTON CANDY

DONUT

ERASER

FLAMINGO

GRAPEFRUIT

HIBISCUS

ICE CREAM
(STRAWBERRY)

JELLO

KERNS GUAVA NECTAR

LEMONADE

MY LITTLE PONY

NUDIBRANCH

ORCHID

PIGLET

QUAIRADING PINK LAKE

ROSE'

SALMON

TAFFY

URCHIN

VALENTINE

WATERMELON

XIGUA

YOGURT

ZINNIA

BLACK...

BLACK

from A to Z

(COLOR THE WORD AND EACH SQUARE BLACK)

ASPHALT

BOWLING BALL

COAL

DARTH VADER

EIGHT BALL

FLAG

GARBAGE BAG

HOLE

INK

JAMAICAN FLAG

KNIGHT

LIMOUSINE

MAMBA

NINJA

OLIVE

PANTHER

QUESTION MARK?

RAVEN

SHARPIE

TIRE

UMPIRE

VULTURE

WITCH

X-RAY

YEMEN FLAG

ZORRO

WHITE...

WHITE
from A to Z

(LEAVE THE WORD AND EACH SQUARE WHITE)
(Or color each square with a white crayon or colored pencil)

AVALANCHE

BASEBALL

CUE BALL

DISH

EGG

FLOUR

GLUE

HORCHATA

IGLOO

JICAMA

KLEENEX

LIGHT BULB

MARSHMALLOW

NURSE

ONION

POLAR BEAR

QUILTED NORTHERN

RICE

SALT

TALCUM POWDER

UNICORN

VANILLA ICE CREAM

WEDDING DRESS

X-MAS STAR

YETI

ZURICH

GRAY...

GRAY

from A to Z

(COLOR THE WORD AND EACH SQUARE GRAY)

ASHES

BATTLESHIP

CEMENT

DUMBBELL

ELEPHANT

FOG

GAMEBOY

HINDENBURG

IRON

JACKRABBIT

KOALA

LINT

MANTA RAY

NICKEL

OSTRICH

PEWTER

QUARTZITE

RHINO

SMOKE

TORNADO

U-BOAT

VOLCANIC ASH

WHALE

XEME

YUCATAN SQUIRREL

ZINC

THE END